LUDWIG VAN BEETHOVEN

PIANO CONCERTO No. 4

G major/G-Dur/Sol majeur
Op. 58

Edited by/Herausgegeben von
Richard Clarke

Ernst Eulenburg Ltd

London · Mainz · Madrid · New York · Paris · Prague · Tokyo · Toronto · Zürich

CONTENTS

BEETHOVEN'S CONCERTO PRODUCTION: COMPOSITION, PERFORMANCE, PUBLICATION
BEETHOVENS KONZERTSCHAFFEN: DATEN DER ENTSTEHUNG, URAUFFÜHRUNG, VERÖFFENTLICHUNG

	Title and key/ Titel und Tonart	(Preliminary) principal dates of composition/ (Entwürfe) Haupt-Kompositionsdaten	First performance/ Uraufführung	First edition/ Erstausgabe (as orch. Parts)	Dedication/ Widmung
Op.19	Piano Concerto No.2, B♭	begun before 1793; rev.1794, 1798	29 March 1795 Vienna	Leipzig, 1801	Carl Nicklas von Nickelsberg
Op.15	Piano Concerto No.1, C	1795; ?rev. 1800	18 Dec 1795 Prague	Vienna, 1801	Fürstin Barbara Odescalchi (née Gräfin von Keglevics)
Op.37	Piano Concerto No.3, C	?1800	5 April 1803 Vienna	Vienna, 1804	Fürst Louis Ferdinand von Preußen
Op.56	Triple Concerto, C Pfte, Vln, Vc, Orch	1803–4	May 1808 Vienna	Vienna, 1807	Fürst Franz Joseph von Lobkowitz
Op.58	Piano Concerto No.4, G	1805–6	March 1807 Vienna	Vienna, 1808	Erzherzog Rudolph von Österreich
Op.61	Violin Concerto, D	1806	23 Dec 1806 Vienna	Vienna, 1808 London, 1810	Stephan von Breuning
Op.73	Piano Concerto No.5, E♭ ('Emperor')	1809	?28 Nov 1811 Leipzig	London, 1810 Leipzig, 1811	Erzherzog Rudolph von Österreich

(List excludes fragments, incomplete works, and soloistic works not titled 'Concerto'/Die Liste beinhaltet keine Fragmente, unvollendete Werke oder solistische Stücke, die nicht mit "Konzert" betitelt sind.)

PREFACE

Beethoven began noting down ideas for his Fourth Piano Concerto early in 1804, around the same time that he began sketching the Fifth Symphony. To give some idea of how active his imagination was during this period, he was also working on his opera *Leonore* (later to be revised as *Fidelio*), while the spring and summer of that year also saw the composition of the Triple Concerto and the F major Piano Sonata, Op.54. The fact that the Fourth Piano Concerto appears to have been conceived concurrently with the Fifth Symphony is especially interesting. Both works begin with what is essentially the same rhythmic figure: short-short-short-long [ᵕᵕᵕ–]; and yet the characters of both these openings present a striking contrast. The Symphony's defiant opening gesture is one of the most arresting in the symphonic repertoire. The Concerto's beginning is no less compelling, but it achieves its effect by stealth: the soloist sounds a gentle G major chord (marked *piano, dolce*), a tiny contemplation of the germinal rhythmic motif follows, then a brief upward run falls quietly onto the dominant, before handing over to the orchestral strings, *pianissimo*.

In performance, the effect of this solo prelude can be like a brief improvisation: a private meditation before the main business of the Concerto begins – rather as in the tiny opening *Adagio cantabile* of the Piano Sonata in F sharp major, Op.78. Yet it is from this seeming forethought that so many of the work's leading ideas and dramatic strokes derive. After prevailing in the first movement the same rhythmic pattern can also be felt – in more jagged dotted form – in the stern opening string motif of the second movement (II: bb1–2), while the piano's decorated version of the finale's first theme (III: bb11–13) is clearly based on the same figure. Just as important is the surprise change of harmony at the first orchestral entry (I: b6): B major after a pause on the dominant of G. This G-B opposition casts a long shadow over the first

movement (e.g. bb40ff, bb204–7, and of course at the beginning of the recapitulation, bb253–258), while the move from the slow movement's E minor tonality to a C major harmony at the beginning of the finale is likewise that of a major third.

Just as seminal however are the ideas of improvisation and gentle reflection set out at the beginning. The piano's first solo entry (b74f) after the orchestral ritornello in the first movement is a long way from the massively assertive running octaves at the equivalent passage in the Third Concerto. The soloist's hushed, at first harmonically ambiguous reflection on the seminal ᵕᵕᵕ – rhythm seems to stop the orchestral tutti in its tracks. Still more arresting is the solo entry that inaugurates the development section (b192): the piano's repeated F naturals (again *piano*) calmly questioning the solid D major of the exposition's *forte* orchestral conclusion and inaugurating some remarkably exploratory piano writing, both in terms of harmony and of tone colour (bb194–203). The piano's lavishly decorated version of the Concerto's opening solo which announces the recapitulation (I: bb 253–7) is another arresting instance: initially triumphal, it quickly fades back to the original *piano, dolce*, now melting into liquid chromatics before the expected pause on the dominant.

It is in the *Andante con moto* however that the idea of lyrical reflection prevailing over powerful orchestral assertion reaches full fruition. In a movement that seems overall more like a wordless operatic *scena* than classical concerto slow movement, the piano responds to the strings' stern octaves with a series of pleading or placatory solos marked *molto cantabile* – the contrast is underlined by Beethoven's instruction to the pianist to use the *una corda* pedal throughout. Comparisons between this dramatic orchestra-soloist dialogue and classical Greek legends of the divine musician Orpheus taming wild beasts or calming the shades in Hades, go back at least to the mid 19th century.[1] While there is no evidence that Beethoven was thinking in such specific mythological terms, the music clearly invites some kind of pictorial – or even philosophical interpretation, especially in the way the piano's lyricism eventually seems to pacify or subdue the orchestra's wrathful motif, which by b64 has been reduced to a *ppp* shadow of its former self.

As Lewis Lockwood has noted, Beethoven's models here were almost certainly the dramatic accompanied recitatives of Mozart:[2] Donna Anna's confrontation with Don Ottavio in Act One of *Don Giovanni*, or the Countess's more private confrontation with her own lonely fate in Act Two of *Figaro*. Beethoven was a master of instrumental recitative, using it to very different effects in the D minor Piano Sonata, Op.31 No. 2, the A minor String Quartet, Op.132, and famously in the finale of the Ninth Symphony. But here the soloist's phrases are neither volatile nor fluid recitative, but balanced, measured lyrical phrases. This device has been imitated by others – most notably by César Franck at the beginning of his *Symphonic Variations*; however there is something about this movement which remains unique, a kind of rarefied musical poetry which is both 'classical' and 'romantic', and yet transcends both. After this the Rondo Finale (which follows without a break) is a release of pent-up energy, though Beethoven's teasing sense of humour is also much in evidence, especially in the way he later exploits the 'wrong key' opening (C major instead of G major) of the Finale theme.

Beethoven completed the Fourth Piano Concerto in early-to-mid 1806, and gave the first private performance in March 1807 at the house of 'Prince L' (accounts are confused as to whether the Prince in question was Lobkowitz or Lichnowsky).[3] The Concerto's public debut – with Beethoven again acting as both soloist and director of the orchestra – took place at a benefit concert arranged by the composer at Vienna's Theater an der Wien on 22 December 1808, and which also included the Fifth and Sixth Symphonies, the *Choral Fantasy*, movements from the *Mass in C*, the concert aria 'Ah, perfido!' and a substantial improvisation by Beethoven at the piano. Despite the length of the programme, inadequate rehearsal and the bitter cold inside the unheated theatre, the Concerto made a very favourable impression. The philosopher, musician and travel writer J.F.Reichardt was present, and described how Beethoven played the Concerto

astonishingly well and at the fastest possible tempos. The Adagio [sic], a masterpiece of beautiful sustained melody, he made his instrument sing with a profound melancholy feeling which awakened a similar response in me.[4]

Stephen Johnson

[1] For a historical summary of these 'Orpheus' readings, see Leon Plantinga, *Beethoven's Concertos: History, Style, Performance* (New York, 1999), 185–194

[2] Lewis Lockwood, *Beethoven: The Music and Life* (New York, 2003), 243–4

[3] See Barry Cooper (ed.): *The Beethoven Compendium* (London, 1991), 18–19

[4] J.F.Reichardt, *Briefe geschrieben auf einer Reise nach Wien* (Amsterdam, 1810), I/257 (author's trans.)

VORWORT

Ungefähr zeitgleich mit dem Beginn seiner Arbeit an der 5. Sinfonie begann Beethoven Anfang 1804, seine Ideen für das 4. Klavierkonzert zu notieren. Zu dieser Zeit war er so kreativ, dass er außerdem noch an seiner Oper *Leonore* (später in *Fidelio* umbenannt) arbeitete und darüber hinaus im Frühjahr und Sommer desselben Jahres das Tripelkonzert sowie die Klaviersonate in F-Dur op. 54 komponierte. Die Tatsache, dass das 4. Klavierkonzert und die 5. Sinfonie anscheinend gleichzeitig entstanden, ist besonders interessant. Beide Werke beginnen im Wesentlichen mit derselben rhythmischen Figur: kurz-kurz-kurz-lang [⌣⌣⌣–], und doch wirken die beiden Einleitungen sehr gegensätzlich. Das markante Anfangsmotiv der Sinfonie gehört zu den faszinierendsten des gesamten sinfonischen Repertoires. Das Klavierkonzert beginnt zwar ebenso fesselnd, erzielt seinen Effekt jedoch durch Zurückhaltung: Der Solist spielt einen leisen G-Dur-Akkord (der mit *piano*, *dolce* bezeichnet ist), gefolgt von einer Andeutung des rhythmischen Anfangsmotivs. Anschließend endet ein kurzer aufsteigender Lauf leise auf der Dominante, bevor die Streicher *pianissimo* einsetzen.

Bei einer Aufführung kann dieses Anfangssolo wie eine kurze Improvisation anmuten: eine persönliche Meditation, bevor der Hauptteil des Konzerts beginnt – ähnlich wie die kurze Einleitung *Adagio cantabile* der Klaviersonate in Fis-Dur op. 78. Und doch werden so viele Hauptthemen und dramatische Wendungen des Werks aus diesem scheinbaren Vordersatz abgeleitet. Das im ersten Satz vorherrschende rhythmische Motiv findet sich – in punktierter Form – im düsteren Anfangsmotiv der Streicher im zweiten Satz (II: Takt 1–2) wieder, und auch die verzierte Klavierversion des ersten Themas aus dem Finale (III: Takt 11–13) baut eindeutig auf derselben Figur auf. Ebenso wichtig ist der überraschende Harmoniewechsel, wenn das Orchester zum ersten Mal einsetzt (I: Takt 6):

H-Dur nach einer Pause auf der Dominante von G. Dieser Kontrast zwischen G-Dur und H-Dur prägt den ersten Satz erheblich (z. B. in Takt 40ff, 204–207 und natürlich zu Beginn der Reprise in Takt 253–258). Beim Wechsel von e-Moll im langsamen Satz zu C-Dur am Anfang des Finales handelt es sich ebenfalls um eine große Terz.

Genauso bahnbrechend sind jedoch die Improvisation und leise Reflexion zu Beginn. Der erste Soloeinsatz des Klaviers (Takt 74f) nach dem Ritornell des Orchesters im ersten Satz ist weit entfernt von den prägnanten Oktavläufen der entsprechenden Passage im 3. Klavierkonzert. Die gedämpfte, harmonisch zunächst unklare Reflexion des zugrunde liegenden ⌣⌣⌣ Rhythmus scheint die orchestralen Tutti zum Stillstand zu bringen. Noch faszinierender ist das Solo, das die Durchführung einleitet (Takt 192): Mit seinen wiederholten Fs (wiederum im *piano*) stellt das Klavier das stabile D-Dur des vom Orchester im *forte* gespielten Schlusses der Exposition infrage und wirkt sowohl harmonisch als auch bezüglich der Klangfarbe bemerkenswert experimentell (Takt 194–203). Die reich verzierte Version des Anfangssolos des Konzerts, die das Klavier als Ankündigung der Reprise (I: Takt 253–257) spielt, ist ein weiterer fesselnder Moment: zunächst triumphal, schwindet sie rasch zum ursprünglichen *piano*, *dolce* und löst sich vor der erwarteten Pause auf der Dominante in eine fließende Chromatik auf.

Erst im *Andante con moto* wird die Idee, dass die lyrische Reflexion über das mächtige Selbstbewusstsein des Orchesters siegt, vollends verwirklicht. In einem Satz, der insgesamt eher wie eine wortlose Opernszene anmutet und nicht so sehr wie der langsame Satz eines klassischen Konzerts, reagiert das Klavier auf die harten Oktaven der Streicher mit einer Reihe flehender, beschwichtigender Soli, die *molto cantabile* gespielt werden – der Kontrast wird durch Beethovens Anweisung an den Pianisten, durchgängig das *una-corda*-Pedal zu verwenden, unterstrichen. Vergleiche zwischen diesen dramatischen Dialogen zwischen Orchester und Solist und dem göttlichen Musiker Orpheus aus der griechischen Mythologie, der wilde Tiere zähmt und die Schatten im Hades beruhigt, entstanden spätestens Mitte des 19. Jahrhunderts.[1] Es gibt zwar keine Belege dafür, dass Beethoven konkret diese Mythologie im Sinn hatte, doch fordert die Musik eine bildliche – oder sogar philosophische – Interpretation geradezu heraus, vor allem, wenn die lyrische Gesinnung des Klaviers schließlich das wütende Motiv des Orchesters besiegt, das in Takt 64 nur noch ein *ppp*-Schatten seiner selbst ist.

Laut Lewis Lockwood dienten Beethoven hier höchstwahrscheinlich Mozarts dramatische, begleitete Rezitative als Vorlage:[2] Donna Annas Konfrontation mit Don Ottavio im ersten Akt von *Don Giovanni* bzw. die ganz persönliche Konfrontation der Gräfin mit ihrem einsamen Schicksal im zweiten Akt des *Figaro*. Beethoven war ein Meister des instrumentalen Rezitativs und erzielte damit in der Klaviersonate in d-Moll op. 31 Nr. 2, dem Streichquartett in a-Moll op. 132 und im berühmten Finale seiner 9. Sinfonie ganz unterschiedliche Effekte. Doch hier sind die Phrasen des Solisten weder sprunghafte noch fließende Rezitative, sondern ausgeglichene, gemessene lyrische Phrasen. Dieses Stilmittel wurde von anderen nachgeahmt, vor allem von César Franck am Anfang seiner *Symphonischen Variationen*. Trotzdem hat dieser Satz etwas ganz Einzigartiges, eine Art verfeinerte musikalische Poesie, die sowohl „klassisch" als auch „romantisch" ist und doch über beides hinausgeht. Anschließend setzt das Finale des Rondos (das ohne Pause folgt) die aufgestaute Energie frei, obgleich Beethovens Sinn für Humor ebenfalls zum Tragen kommt, vor allem in der Art und Weise, wie er später das Thema des Finales in der „falschen Tonart" (C-Dur anstatt G-Dur) beginnen lässt.

Beethoven vollendete das 4. Klavierkonzert zwischen Anfang und Mitte 1806 und spielte es erstmals im März 1807 im privaten Rahmen im Haus von „Fürst L" (in der Literatur herrscht Verwirrung darüber, ob es sich bei dem betreffenden Fürsten um Lobkowitz oder Lichnowsky handelte).[3] Die öffentliche Uraufführung des Konzerts – ebenfalls mit Beethoven als Solist und Orchesterleiter – fand im Rahmen eines Benefizkonzerts statt, das der Komponist am 22. Dezember 1808 am Theater an der Wien veranstaltete und bei dem auch die 5. und 6. Sinfonie, die *Chorfantasie*, Sätze aus der *Messe C-Dur*, die Konzertarie „Ah, perfido!" sowie eine längere Improvisation von Beethoven am Klavier zu hören waren. Trotz der Länge des Programms, unzureichender Proben und der bitteren Kälte im unbeheizten Theater fand das Konzert großen Anklang. Der Philosoph, Musiker und Reiseschriftsteller J. F. Reichardt war dort. Laut seiner Beschreibung spielte Beethoven das Konzert

zum Erstaunen brav, in den allerschnellsten Tempis […]. Das Adagio, ein Meistersatz von schönem durchgeführtem Gesange, sang er wahrhaft auf seinem Instrumente mit tiefem melancholischem Gefühl, das auch mich dabei durchströmte.[4]

Stephen Johnson
Übersetzung: Heike Brühl

---

[1] Eine historische Zusammenfassung der „Orpheus"-Lektüre befindet sich in Leon Plantingas *Beethoven's Concertos: History, Style, Performance* (New York, 1999), S. 185–194.

[2] Lewis Lockwood, *Beethoven: The Music and Life* (New York, 2003), S. 243–244.

[3] Siehe Barry Cooper (Hg.): *The Beethoven Compendium* (London, 1991), S. 18–19.

[4] J. F. Reichardt, *Briefe geschrieben auf einer Reise nach Wien* (Amsterdam, 1810), I/S. 57.

PIANO CONCERTO No. 4

Dem Erzherzog Rudolph von Österreich gewidmet

Ludwig van Beethoven
(1770–1827)
Op. 58

I. Allegro moderato

© 2010 Ernst Eulenburg Ltd, London
and Ernst Eulenburg & Co GmbH, Mainz

No. 705   EE 3805

3

12

18

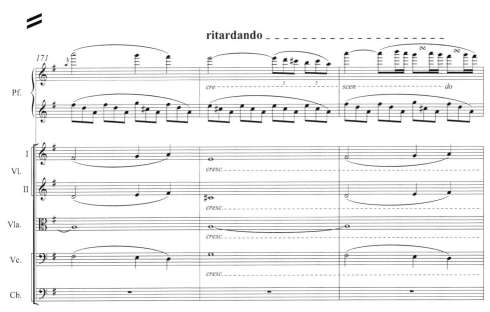

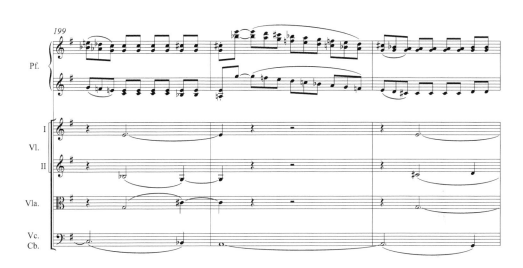

32

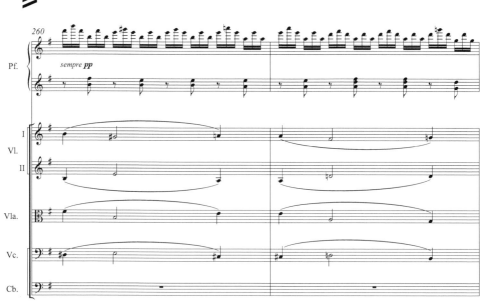

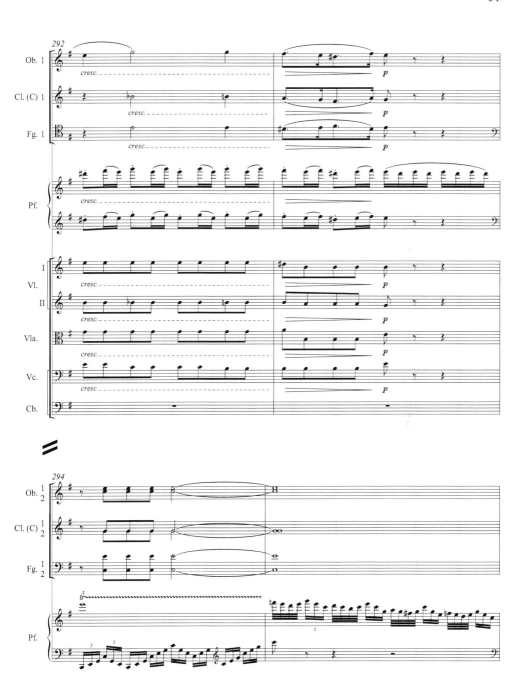

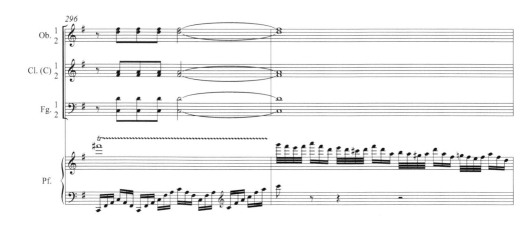

Cadenza *)

62

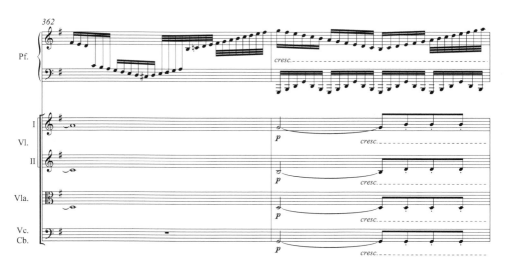

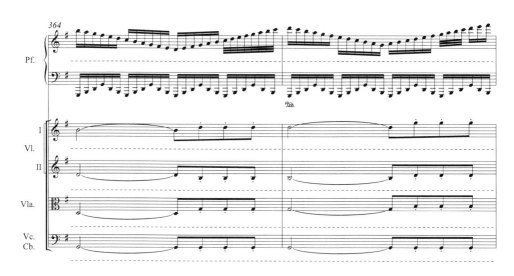

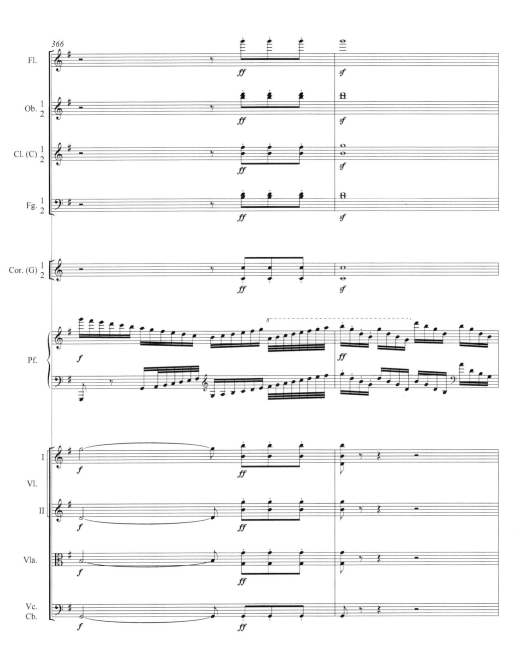

II. Andante con moto

*) 'Dan[s] tout cet Andante on tient levée la Pédale, qui ne fait sonner qu'une corde. Au signe Ped. on leve outre cela les étouffoirs.'

III. Rondo
Vivace

72

85

108

112

*) see appendix

120

Appendix: Beethoven's Cadenzas

Two Cadenzas to the first movement, bar 346

(a) **Allegro**

Tempo primo

(b)

128

ritardando ‑ ‑ ‑ ‑ ‑ ‑ ‑ ‑ ‑ ‑

‑ ‑ ‑ ‑ ‑ ‑ ‑ ‑ ‑ ‑ **Tempo I**

Poco sostenuto

Tempo moderato   **Presto**

(c) Cadenza to the third movement, bar 499